Stir Your Soul!

INSPIRATIONS FOR YOU TO DREAM, GROW AND LIVE BOLDLY

DARLENE BURGESS DAVIS

Copy Editor – Skye Loyd

Cover Design – Euan Monaghan

ISBN: 978-1-7342448-0-9

THIS BOOK IS DEDICATED TO

God,
who is in charge.

My husband, Fred,
who lets me run with all of my ideas, even the crazy ones.

My children, grandchildren, and one great-grandchild,
who I'm proud to say are mine.

My sisters,
who have encouraged and listened to me every week for
months.

Table of Contents

MOTIVATION

ENCOURAGEMENT

LOVE

FAITH

BLESSINGS

GOD CAN

GUIDANCE

THE WORD OF GOD

GIVE THANKS

TRUST

MY THOUGHTS

HOLIDAYS

Motivation

ARE YOU READY?

Are you ready to get out of bed and seize the day,
Seize your morning, time, and schedule?
Begin by thanking God for all your blessings:
For waking up, for family, health, home, food, and clothing.
Follow up with a few minutes of stretching and exercising to
honor and take care of your temple.
Spend a few moments reading. Listen to something
inspirational, to catapult you into the day.
Do something that will help you spring into action.
Achieve the desires of your heart and chip away at the ideas in
your mind.
If you have ups or downs, happiness or sadness thrust at you,
find joy and peace within.
Find a spark to light your fire, to move you to action and to
keep you going.
Are you ready to live and to do so more abundantly?
If so, you must move your mind, heart, hands, and feet.
Faith without works is dead.
Get yourself moving to the life that you desire.

If you aren't ready, it's time to get ready.

BELIEVE - NO. 1

Believe in God,
He is the giver of life and the abundant life you seek.

Believe in Jesus,
He is God's precious son and our brother who died for us,
To give eternal life.

Believe in the Holy Spirit,
Our heavenly guide, our comforter,
Our teacher and our director.

Believe in yourself,
God made you in His image,
Reflecting His nature,
To be the master
Of all life on earth, sky, and sea.

He blessed you and said,
Prosper!
Reproduce!
Fill the earth!
Take charge!

If you believe in the Father, Jesus the Son, and the Holy Spirit
you can do anything.

Why aren't you receiving?
Why aren't you reproducing or prospering?
Is it because you don't believe?

All you need is the faith of a mustard seed and you can move mountains.

You can do all things, but only if you B-E-L-I-E-V-E – Believe.

WE RISE UP!

We rise up
When we are told no, no, and no again.
You can't do that,
It can't be done.

We rise up
When we have our goals and mission in life
In front of us.

We rise up
When we see our vision
And look at our vision board every day.

We rise up
When our dreams are as real during the day as they are at
night.

We rise up
When we not only see our aspirations,
But we can taste them as well.

We rise up
When we know nothing is impossible.

We rise up
When we remember that miracles
Are happening around us every single day.

We rise up
Because we know
Without a vision we will perish.

We rise up
When we realize, that we need to ask and receive,
But hard work is a part of the equation.

We rise up
When we work beyond our own doubt
And the doubt and criticism of others.

We rise up
When we trust and believe.

We rise up
When we do our best every time,
For everyone, in every situation.

We rise up
When we humble ourselves.

We rise up
When we love and give.

We rise up
When we just try.

We rise up
When we lend a helping hand.

We rise up
When we look for the positive solution
And not everything that can go wrong.

We rise up
When we embrace laughter.

We rise up
When we see the possibilities.

We rise up
When we read and pray.

We rise up
When we allow a little flexibility
And open our heart and mind for change.

We rise up
When we are ready to rise.

Yes, we rise up!

JOURNEY

Are you on a journey?
Or are you standing still?
Are you flying, walking, or crawling?
Are you joyful or miserable?
Are you living your best life or barely living?
Do you give, or do you squeeze the life out of what you have?
Are you anticipating or dissipating?
Are you soaring, or are you still trying to sort it out?
Where are you on your life's journey,
At the beginning,
In the middle,
Or close to the end?
Regardless of where you are on your journey,
Keep it moving,
Keep it real
And keep it you.
Only you can walk your journey.
Journey on.

FREE ME

Is your mind screaming to be delivered
To be set free from the noise and chatter
That have invaded you?
Telling you
It's too much
I can't take it anymore
I'm tired
I need a break
I can't do this
I can't do this alone
I've had enough
I'm the poorest person in the group
My house is the worst looking house on the block
I don't have enough
I think I should remove myself from the equation
Then everybody would be better off without me
I'm the problem
I'm the holdup
I think I'm losing my mind
I don't want to hurt anyone
Things are spinning out of control
I don't know what to do
I wish I could. . . .
How do I stop the noise?
How do I stop the chatter?

Stop
Acknowledge the mind storm
Sit
Close your eyes
Breathe

Inhale through your nose
Exhale through your mouth
You determine how long you need to sit and breathe
One minute, ten, an hour, or a day
Take the time
Sit, breathe, relax your mind and your body
Once you're relaxed and calm enough
Go about your day

If need be, find other things that will relax you
Listen to some music, pray,
Read a good uplifting book or the Bible,
Cook, bake, sew, sing, dance, go fishing,
Call someone who you know will support you,
Work in your garden, take a walk, exercise,
Get a hot or cold drink, take a shower, take a nap,
Draw, color, write,
Do something that will get you over and through this state
Get a good night's sleep

When you wake up, repeat if necessary
For as many times as you need to
If you think you need counseling,
Please get counseling right away
Be important to yourself
Do something every day
For you only, to make you smile
To make you free

IT'S HARD

It's hard to wake up in the morning
When you feel like
You don't have a reason to get up.

It's hard to face
Family and friends
When you have conned,
Cheated, scammed, and lied
To them for so long.
You don't think they
Will ever trust you again.

It's hard to look in the mirror
At yourself,
When you have
Neglected and abused
Your body
For years
And allowed others to do so as well.

It's hard to love
Or even like yourself,
When you think you're
So repulsive and unworthy
Of anything good.

It's hard, but you can live again.
You can wake up
And realize how much you have to live for.

Your family and friends
Can learn to trust you.

You can look in the mirror
And love
Who you see
And who you have become.

It's hard.
It's going to take some work,
But nothing is impossible.
Believe that you can do it.
Tell yourself that you can.
Pray and ask God to help you.
Go to church.
Join a support group.
Change your circle of friends.
Change your activities.
Find fun things to do.
Challenge yourself every day.
Believe in yourself every day.
Set small goals that you can accomplish.
Believe in yourself some more.
Pray some more.

It's hard,
But you'll get there.
And as time goes on
It will get easier
Keep on pushing and always be thankful.

CLOCK

Tick tock goes the clock,
The clock that tracks the seconds, minutes, and hours of a day.

Tick tock goes the biological clock,
The system in the body that controls the occurrence of natural processes
(Sleeping and aging)
Psychological processes
(Learning, perception, language, thought, attention, memory, motivation, and emotion)
And the cyclical behavior
(Behavior that occurs in a regular cycle, a regular pattern).

Tick tock goes the clock
For opportunities presenting themselves, doors opening and closing.

Tick tock goes the clock
For seasons, favor, blessings, and direction.

Are you paying attention to the clock on the wall,
Or the clock in your mind and your body?

Do you hear the tick tock of the opportunities,
The doors,
The seasons,
The blessings,
The direction,
And changes?

Hear the tick, listen to the tock
And put yourself in motion
To live and receive
Before your clocks stop ticking and tocking.

Tick Tock

I CAN'T BELIEVE IT,
I WON'T BELIEVE IT

I can't believe
You are talking to me
Like I'm a dog or tramp.
I won't believe
You're the best I can do.

I can't believe
That you stole
My money, pride, and dignity.
I won't believe
That I have to stay broke
And stripped of my dignity and pride.

I can't believe
You hit me so hard
That I fell and broke my arm.
I won't believe
That because you hit me
I can't get up,
Not only get up,
But thrive and use that arm
To go further than even
I could have imagined.

I can't believe
You went behind my back
And said such vicious
And mean things about me.
I won't believe

That your words define me
Or my character.

I can't believe
You told those boldfaced lies about me.
I won't believe
A word that you spoke about me,
But I will let your evil words
Fuel my fire to speak my truth.

I can't believe
You took pictures with that person
And put it on Facebook.
I won't believe that this face
Is incapable of finding the
Right person to see me.

I will believe
I can make it without you,
I can soar and rise above it all.
I can do my thing and
Do it with a spirit of excellence.

I will believe
I am somebody
And somebody special to a special somebody.
I can reach my destiny
And fulfill my purpose in life.
I can enjoy my life,
Do me and be me.

I will believe
Everything I touch will grow
Everyone I meet will be encouraged
And everything I do will be successful.

What?

I didn't hear you.
I can't believe
You are telling me
That you love me.
I definitely won't believe a word you are saying.
I won't ever believe
That I can't make it without you,
Because I can, and I believe that!

I SAID TO MYSELF - NO. 1

I said to myself,
Self, what do you want to be when you grow up?
Self said to me,
Aren't you already grown?
What are you waiting for?

I said to myself,
Self, we are going to start on our journey for good health
tomorrow,
Eating more fruits and vegetables,
Cutting back on the carbs and sugar,
And exercising at least 15 minutes a day.
Self said to me,
You said that five years ago,
A year ago,
Even last week.
What are you waiting for?

I said to myself,
Self, we are going to learn a new language.
Self said to me,
A qué estàs esperando? (*What are you waiting for?* in Spanish)
and Qu'attends-tu? (*What are you waiting for?* in French)

I said to myself,
Self, we are going to ask for a promotion.
Self said to me,
I thought you were going to do that last month.
What are you waiting for?

I said to myself,
Self, I'm not going to take any more mistreatment.
Self said to me,
I've heard that before.

I said to myself,
Self, we have to be more productive and use our time wisely.
Self said to me,
Didn't you say that five hours ago
Before you turned on the computer?

I said to myself,
Self, I'm going to get on top of things right now,
Being what I'm supposed to be,
Starting my journey to excellent health,
Learning that new language,
Asking for the promotion,
Not taking any abusive treatment—mental, physical, or
verbal—
And using my time wisely.

Self said to me,
Whenever you're ready I got your back.
I'm here for you,
Don't wait any longer.
I said to myself, Let's do it!

I SAID TO MYSELF - NO. 2

I said to myself,
Self, what are you afraid of?
Why are you rushing?
Why are you worried about what they think?
Why does that even matter?
Why do you doubt yourself, your skills, and your wisdom?
Why do you care?
Why is that important?
Why is that important to you?
Why does that concern you?
Is that your concern?
How does that concern you?
Why do you abuse your body?
Why don't you pay attention to the signs?
Why do you overeat?
Why do you eat when you know you just finished eating?
Why do you eat when you're not hungry?
Why do you doubt others?
Why don't you trust your instinct?
Why do you let others interfere?
What is it going to take?
When are you going to believe in yourself?
When will you see your worth?
Why don't you think you're good enough or smart enough?
When will you let it go?
Why can't you trust?
Will you ever trust anyone again?
What's the big deal?
When are you going to slow down?
When are you going to stop?
What's the problem?

What's wrong?
Why don't you let it go?
Who said that's true?
Why do you believe that?
Why do you have to prove yourself?
Why do you have to convince them, him, or her?
Why can't that wait?
Why don't you let that wait?
What's that to you?
Why can't you call them later?
Who said that and what makes you think it's true?
Why are you so angry?
Why are you so downcast and unhappy?
Why are you so stressed?
Why are you trippin'?
Why don't you take it easy?
When are you going to rest?
When will you get it together?
When will you start?
When will you stop?
When is enough enough?
How many times do you have to hear it?
When will you let bygones be bygones?
When will you realize the possibilities?
How can you help somebody?
How can you win?
How can you move forward?

I said to myself, "How, when, what, and why?
Self said, I don't have all of the answers,
But the questions are certainly making me think and
Realize that we have some changes to make
And we need to start right now.

READY OR NOT - NO. 1

Whether you are ready or not, life is going to happen.
Things are going to go wrong.
People are going to talk about you,
Treat you badly, discredit, and diss you.

Ready or not, you are going to get older.
You may gain or lose weight.
Your skin may sag in various places.
Your steps may become slow and your stride may shorten.
Your vision may dim and your hearing dampen.

Ready or not, time will pass you by—
The seconds, minutes, hours, days, and years;
Winter, spring, summer, and fall.
Opportunities will come and go, and windows will close.

Ready or not, there will be a time to die.
So please don't let life pass you by
While you mull over and count the things that went wrong,
The people who have insulted, discredited, and used you.

As you lose weight, hearing, sight, the length of your stride,
Skin elasticity, or the quickness of your steps,
Don't let the minutes and opportunities pass,
Because the windows and the seasons will come and go.

During your lifetime make sure you try,
Explore the possibilities,
Have fun,
Give it something, if not your all,

Make your life meaningful and let it stand for what you believe.

Live while you are alive,
Because one day you will die,

Ready or not.

READY OR NOT - NO. 2

Whether you are ready or not,
Life is going to happen.
If you are not careful
It will pass you by.

One day you will look up and say,
Where did the time go?
What have I done with my life?
What did I accomplish?

Who did I help?
Was I happy?
Did I bring joy to anyone?

If you don't like the answers
To your questions,
Look around and see what you can do
For a better outcome.
Because ready or not,
Life is going to happen.

WAKE UP!

Why are you still asleep?
You want to be something in life.
You want to make a difference in the world.
You want to be a millionaire.
Your dream is to go to the pros,
Be an NBA star.

Why are you still in bed?
You want to travel and
See this magnificent world.
You have inventions inside of you.
You have business ideas swirling around in your head.

You want to get a job?
Wake up!
You want to go to college?
Wake up!

Whatever you want to do,
Big or small,
You can't do it
If you're still asleep,
If you're wrapped up in your sheets,
Or if your mind is wrapped up in
Fear, doubt, unbelief,
Or just the wrong things.

Wake up!
Wake up!
It will only happen
When you wake up.

THIS LITTLE...

This little life of mine
    is worth living and living to the full,
    abundantly, bravely, boldly, confidently,
    and out loud.

This little tongue of mine
    is going to speak,
    but speak truthfully,
    at all times,
    at the appropriate time,
    when necessary,
    without hesitation,
    and, if called for, out loud.

This little mind of mine
    is going to think,
    think of creative ideas, businesses, and inventions,
    as well as ways to help and bless others.

These little hands of mine
    are going to put into action
    and accomplish the creative ideas,
    businesses, and inventions.

These little feet of mine
    are going to be swift to run and do good,
    to help and give a hand up.

This little heart of mine
    is going to love,
    love everybody,

regardless of race,
status in life,
location,
or their love for me.

This little heart was broken,
but love won't let it stay that way,
won't let it get bitter,
full of unforgiveness,
or hatred.

This little heart is made to love,
and that's what it's going to do forever.

DOES IT MATTER?

Does it matter that I don't wear the latest fashions
Or the latest sneakers?
Does it matter that I don't drive a fine car
Or live in a big house?
Does it matter that I didn't go to college,
Or that I went but didn't graduate?
Does it matter that you don't think I'm cute, handsome, or
attractive?
Does it matter that I'm not thin?
Does it matter that I don't have a job that pays a lot of money
Or that I don't have my own business?
Does it matter that I'm not a Hollywood movie star,
That I'm not rich or famous?
Does it matter that I'm not one of the in-crowd?
Does it matter that I'm black, white, American, Chinese,
Japanese, or something else?

No, it doesn't matter, if you're doing your best,
Striving to be the best you and taking care of health, heart, and
home.
No, it doesn't matter, if you are satisfied with your life,
environment, and place on this earth,
Not if you are doing what you think is best for you and for your
family.
No, it doesn't matter, if you are giving your all and living your
best life.

But if you desire to have the latest fashions, sneakers,
a fine car,
A big house, an education, to be thinner-cuter-healthier,

A high-paying job, or your own business, guess what?
You are going to have to work for it, work at it, and work on it.

It's not going to happen overnight.
You can't expect to win the lottery and have everything that
you desire.
It could happen, but the chances are very slim.
So roll up your sleeves and get to work.
Make some calls, read, research, write your ideas down so you
don't forget them.
Talk to people to get information, subscribe to some
magazines.
And yes, you can still go to your local library.
Pray and ask God for wisdom and direction,
Do more listening and less talking,
Stop judging and criticizing,
See the good in yourself and others.
Stop believing that you can't,
Because you can do all things as God gives you strength.

As a man thinketh, so is he.
Either way, it's okay, because it's your life.
Choose and be happy, because you deserve what makes you
happy.
But don't mistreat or destroy anyone to get there.
Yes, it matters

WHO ARE YOU?

Who are you?

A mom, dad, grandma or granddad, an aunt, uncle, sister, brother, sister-in-law, brother-in-law, nephew, niece, half-brother, step-brother, foster mom or dad, great niece, husband, wife, partner, sibling, first or second cousin, fourth cousin once removed, grandson, granddaughter, great-grandmother, great-great-grandfather.

A man, woman, boy, girl, child, newborn, toddler, teenager, young adult, adolescent, lad, middle-aged man, old man, old woman, senior citizen, adult, grownup.

Are you single, married, engaged, separated, divorced, widowed, a bride, groom, best man, maid of honor, grass widow, grass widower, gay, straight, lesbian, transgender or bisexual?

Are you a nanny, teacher, butcher, baker, candlestick maker, banker, teller, clerk or secretary, receptionist, pawn broker, librarian, entrepreneur, farmer, engineer, packer, picker, miner, meter reader, chef, agent, barber, coordinator, dentist, writer, midwife, technician, artist, police, bartender, hairdresser, waiter, veteran, guard, firefighter, pilot, poet or carpenter?

Are you black, white, Asian, Negroid, Caucasoid, Mongoloid, Australoid, Democrat, Republican, Progressive, Communist, Libertarian, Socialist, Green, or Reformed?

Are you a child of God, a saint, a sinner, a liar, a backslider, an upstanding citizen, a crook?

31

Do you know who you are?
Do you have a choice of who you are and who you want to be?
Do you get to decide, pick, and plan your future?
Have you ever tried, or do you just let life happen?
Who would you be, if you could choose?
Does being you cause sheer misery?
What would you do?
Would you be happy doing that?

You are excellent, and you are enough.
You are unique, talented, smart, cute, gorgeous,
Funny, fun and so much more.
Let your light shine.
Bring the gifts out.
Let your beauty show, by being you.
Do you have faults? Yes.
Do you have things that you need to improve?
Absolutely.
But don't let that stop you from being great
And great at what you do.
Still in all, work to improve.
Get help if you need to,
But be the best mom, dad, teenager, artist,
Democrat, Republican, or whoever you are.
Live and enjoy life.
Don't hurt or use people for your betterment.
Help those whom you've been assigned to help.
Do you, be you.
Who are you?

Encouragement

HOLD ON - NO. 1

When you hear the words "Hold on," what do you think about?
Hold on to your hat, your money, your man or woman,
Your integrity or self-respect,
Your seat (you may be in for the ride of your life),
Hope (the only thing you have),
Your dreams (something to live and strive for).
Hold on to your faith and God.
They will get you through it all.

So just hold on.

HOLD ON - NO. 2

Hold on to your dreams.
It's the only way for them to come true.

Hold on to your memories of the good times.
They may be the only thing that can carry you right now.

Hold on to your dignity.
There will be times when you are the only one believing and
respecting you.

Hold on to your family and friends.
No man is an island.

Hold on to your peace.
It is peace that will get you through today.

Hold on to your God.
It is God who will help you hold on to your dreams, memories,
dignity, family, friends, and peace.

Hold on, I say, hold on.

BELIEVE - NO. 2

Believe in yourself.
Believe that you can do it.
You can make it.
You can go there.
You can reach it.
You can achieve it.
You can have it.
You can create it.
You can master it.
You can climb it.
You can move it.
You can start.
You can jump it.
You can open or close it.
You can finish it and you can win.
If only you just believe.

MAKE TODAY THE DAY

Make today the day for you to
Soar
Learn
Grow
Live
Be your best self
Thrive
And give.
Make today the day.

YES, YOU CAN

Yes, you can be great,
Somebody is watching you,
Which is causing them
To grow, strive, and work harder.

Yes, you can do
What you set your mind to do,
You don't waste time or energy.

Yes, you can be a beast,
A person of excellence,
Because you are giving
Your blood, sweat, and tears.

Yes, you can live a victorious life,
You know the victor,
You are not a victim.

Yes, you can make it,
You are a fighter,
Not a quitter.

Yes, you can,
Yes, you will,
And you must get it done,
For everyone coming along beside you,
behind you
And yes, for yourself.
Yes, you can!

IT'S YOURS

It's yours for the asking.
It's yours for the working, giving, taking, and believing.
It's yours for the endurance of pain.
It's yours for the patience and stability.
It's yours for the love.
It's yours for the pleasure and enjoyment.

What's yours?
Whatever you need,
Whatever you want,
And whatever you desire.

What do you have to do?
You have to
Work
Sweat
Try
Believe
Strive
Climb
Rest
Try again
Work some more
Give
Endure
Love
And hold on until it becomes your reality.

For real, it's yours.

THIS IS THE DAY

Psalm 118:24 says,
"This is the day which the Lord hath made;
We will rejoice and be glad in it."
"The Lord has done it this very day;
Let us rejoice today and be glad."
This is also the day for you to
Try and try harder
And if necessary,
Try longer.

Don't give up or quit.
Hang on in there.
Endure the scorn.
Endure the hardship.
Endure the pressure, criticism, condemnation,
Judgment, laughter, taunting, mistakes,
And shortage
(of finances, sleep, help, friends, or motivation).

Endure everything that's coming your way
And telling you to quit,
It's too much and too hard,
You can't do this.

Push, push on through the pressure.
Push on through the pain,
Fatigue,
Through being weary and spent.

Push on through the tears,
Because you can do it.

You can do all things
Because God is,
And He will give you even more strength.

You are going to wait upon the Lord
Who will renew your strength,
You will mount up with wings as eagles,
You will run and not be weary,
You will walk and not faint.

This is the day that the Lord hath made for you to:
Win
Soar
Endure
Show up and show out
Come through with flying colors
Give, sow, and reap
Rejoice
See the miracles
Pray
Praise
Pull yourself up by the bootstraps
Wipe away those tears
Encourage somebody else
Testify
Sing
Dance
And live!
Because this is the day that the Lord hath made.

YOU NEVER

You never tell me I'm pretty
I like your outfit
Your hair looks nice
You smell good
I love gazing at your beauty
You're so smart
You can throw down in the kitchen
Dinner was delicious
You are so organized
I love watching you work your magic
You're so kind and considerate
You're such a giving person
You add so much to my life
I'm glad that God put us together
You are such a good money manager

Well, if you never tell me any of these things it's OK
Because I'm going to tell myself.
What you don't say
Can't overshadow what I believe,
For what I believe becomes my reality and my truth.
As a man thinketh, so is he.
You never, but I tell myself that I am, so I am.
So, though you never, I still am.

WORD

What is the one word that
    you need to focus on, meditate on
    and hold in your heart today?

Is it *peace*,
    because you need God's peace that
    surpasses all human understanding?

Is it *hope*,
    because you are feeling hopeless
    and you can't even think straight?

Is it *love*,
    because you don't feel like you are capable of loving
     anybody today,
    not even yourself
    and you're sure nobody loves you?

Is it *joy*,
    because you don't have any
    and you've heard that He's the joy of your salvation?

Is it *friend*,
    because you lost yours
    and we know Jesus is a brother and friend?

Is it *bread*,
    because the word says,
    "Give us this day our daily bread,"
    or because Jesus said, "I am the bread of life;
    he that cometh to Me shall never hunger?"

Is your word *life*,
  because the Bible says, "I am come that you might have life
  and that you might have it more abundantly"
  or because it says, "Choose life?"

As my pastor, Janet Hellner-Burris, says,
  "What is your one word to hold in your heart today or this
  week?"

Pick that word,
  hide it in your heart to bring you peace, hope, joy, life, and
  love.

Word

GET READY, GET SET, GO!

Get ready, get set, go!

Get ready to have an amazing day.
Set your mind to have it,
Then go and allow it to come to pass.

Get ready to be blessed beyond your wildest dreams.
Set your mind, heart, and hands to receive it,
Then receive it.

Get ready to be the best you.
Set your mind and see it in your mind's eye,
Then go and do it and be it.

Get ready to share your gift with the world.
Set yourself to know that you have something to share,
Then share and give.

Get ready to make some changes.
Get set on the follow-through,
Then follow it through till the end.

Get ready, get set, go.
If you get ready, get set, and go,
Your life can be amazing.

So, get ready, get set, and go!

YOU BETTER KNOW!

You better know.
You are somebody great.
You're wonderful, funny, smart, fun, intelligent,
Beautiful inside and out,
And a terrific human being.

You better know.
You can accomplish
Whatever you set your mind to do.
With faith,
Hard work,
And determination,
You can do it.

You better know.
Someone is waiting to meet you.
It is your destiny for you to meet them
And say a kind word,
Give a hand up,
Or be a friend during a trying and difficult situation.

You better know.
The world is better because you exist.
You are here to fulfill your assignment,
Be it a mom, dad, teacher,
Whatever, whoever,
Contributing to the world.

You better know.
We are all created equally.
We have different shades and hues, different sizes and shapes,

Crafts, gifts, languages and voices,
But we all have a purpose.

You better know.
To be alive is an amazing and miraculous gift.
Regardless of the minor setbacks and problems that you face.

You better know.
It is good to give thanks to the Lord for your being,
Recognizing life as a gift.
Be thankful for your accomplishments, assignment, favor, and health.

You better know.
If you can help someone,
Help them to know what they don't know.

ONCE UPON A TIME

Once upon a time,
You were born.

Once upon a time,
You grew up and did a lot of amazing things.

Once upon a time,
You got your first job and first pay.

Once upon a time,
You met the person of your dreams,
Fell in love, got married, and had a family.

Once upon a time,
You gave your all and now you are
Living your best life.

Some time,
You will come to the end of your journey,
The journey called life.

So, make the most of all times.

Once upon a time.

WHAT ARE YOU GOING TO DO?
WHAT ARE YOU GOING TO SAY?

What are you going to do
When a golden opportunity presents itself?
Will you say I can't handle this?
This is so unexpected.
I'm not ready.
Is this for real?

What are you going to do
When what you thought was a sure thing falls apart and blows
up in your face?
I didn't ask for this.
I'm done.
I've tried everything.
I can't do this.

What are you going to do and what are you going to say
When the person you love doesn't even seem to know that
you are alive?
Instead, someone else says I love you, but you don't love
them.

What are you going to do and say
When tragedy knocks on your front door,
Comes in without an invitation, and bowls you down?
What are you going to do
When everything that you have worked so hard for
Crumbles all around you
And goes up in smoke right before your eyes?
What will you say?

What are you going to say
When sickness attacks your body,
Affects your mind, and eats at the core of your very soul?
What will you do?

Do you give up?
Do you give in?
Do you let it roll off your mind, body, and soul?
Do you shake it off and keep it moving?
It's up to you, you have choices.

You can do this,
You can be strong,
You can stand tall,
You can overcome,
You can carry on and go further.
You can resist the temptation to give up.
You can fight and you can win!

What are you going to do?
What are you going to say?

Love

DO YOU CARE?

Do you care about anybody besides yourself?
Do you help anybody that could use a hand?
Or is it just about you?
Do you watch people struggle and not offer help?
Do you listen if someone needs an ear to bend
Or a shoulder to cry on?
Do you keep all of your time, energy, and resources
In the reservoir for when you may need them,
For a rainy day?

Are you thinking, If I don't take care of myself,
No one else will?

The truth is,
When you help others
With a pure motive,
With no expectation to be paid back,
You'll get it back when you least expect it,
But when you need it the most.

Don't neglect yourself,
And always put others' needs before yours.
But a little caring for someone
Other than yourself
Goes a long way.

Do you care?
Even just a little?

HAVE I TOLD YOU?

Have I told you
How beautiful you are and how wonderful you smell?

Have I told you
What perfection I see when I gaze upon you
And when the words from your lips fall on my ears,
What comfort that I feel?

Did I tell you
How satisfied I am when I sit at the dinner table or lie on our
bed?

Have I mentioned
The courage, boldness, and confidence that I have when I'm in
your presence?

Did I tell you
How that smile of yours lights up the room and my heart,
simultaneously?

Have I told you
That you are the only one for me
And that I don't know
What I would do, who I would be, or where I would be
If you weren't here?

Okay, some of those words
I haven't said lately,
And some of the words I've never spoken at all.
Consider yourself served with
My love, appreciation, thanksgiving,

Gratitude, support, service, encouragement,
Kindness, sincerity, praise, prayers,
Acceptance, generosity, friendship,
And my heart.

Faith

MUSTARD SEED FAITH

The mustard seed is one of the smallest seeds,
But it can grow up to nine feet tall.

Faith is when you believe in something;
You have complete trust or confidence in someone or
something;
You depend on, rely on, expect, or hope for it,
Even if you can't see anything.

Put a little mustard seed faith into action,
Then see miracles and results.

The Bible says, with mustard seed faith,
You can say to a mountain,
Move from here to there, and it will move.
Nothing will be impossible for you.

Your mountain may be
Getting out of the bed in the morning.
Speak to it and get up.

Your mountain may be
Making a phone call,
Starting a business,
Speaking up about a situation,
Writing a book,
Taking a class,
Or moving to a new location.
Speak to the situation.

To see results,
You have to do something.
The Bible says, faith without works is dead.

When you speak to the mountain,
You have to expect, hope, and trust.
You have to move your feet,
Use your mind and hands,
See, feel, then receive,
Knowing that you are worthy to do so.

It's only mustard seed faith.

BELIEVE IN MIRACLES

Believe in miracles,
For it's the only way for them to come true.
Believe in your dreams,
And it won't be just a shut-eye experience.
Believe in your gifts and talents,
And get busy showing the world.
Believe in yourself,
So you can believe in all of the above.
Do you believe in miracles?

ALL YOU CAN DO,
IS ALL YOU CAN DO

All you can do
   is all you can do,
   depending on how you look at it.

If you do all you can do,
   with your strength and wit,
   then that's all you can do.

But if you put God's super and your natural together,
   all you can do
   is not all you can do.

You have gifts and talents,
   strength, wisdom,
   forgiveness, love, joy,
   and peace in you
   that you can't see
   or begin to understand.

Reach out and let God take your hand;
   he can lead you
   and take you to places
   that you can't even imagine.

Don't let all you can do be all that you do.

Blessings

COUNT YOUR BLESSINGS

Do you count your blessings?
How many have you counted?
What were the blessings:
Waking up, food, clothing, shelter,
And other things which we take for granted.

Everybody didn't wake up,
Some don't have food,
Proper clothing, or shoes.
Some slept under a bridge,
That's where they woke up.

Do you count the blessings
Of income, family, friends,
Living in a country with so many liberties,
Time, the seasons, the sun, moon,
and the stars, which all have a purpose?

Are you counting yourself
As one of those blessings?
Figuring out your purpose?

Count it all joy and a blessing:
The good, the bad, and what looks ugly,
Because it's all designed
For your betterment and growth.

When you count the sunrises and sunny days,
Count the dark days and the storms.

When you count the days that are peachy
And all are speaking well of you,
Count the ones when the backbiters
Are out in full force.

When you count the day that you were hired,
Also count the day
When you were let go and told,
Your services are no longer needed.

So the next time you count your blessings,
Count everything as a blessing,
Being worked out for your good.

Make sure you count all your blessings.

ANGELS

Angels all around us fly.
Angels sit with us unbeknownst,
Even when we cry.

Angels are heavenly beings.
Angels are the human beings that we know:
A neighbor, spouse, or friend,
An angel till the end.

Do angels fly, walk, or crawl?
Do you recognize their presence when in a brawl?
They come to rescue you
Or render service you may need,
Without which, you couldn't succeed.

So, when your angel walks, crawls, or flies by,
Don't be weary and cease the cry.

You can make it, yes you can.
Especially if you are somebody's angel and lending them a
hand.

HELLO, WORLD

Hello, world.
What do you know?
What do you think?
What do you think about?
It's a new day,
Every time you wake up in the morning.

What will you do
With your golden ticket today?
Use every ounce of this day,
To make, help, or allow something good to happen
In your life and in the lives of others.

JUST ME

Just me sitting here, alone,
  thinking about the many blessings that I've had in my life
  and wondering what I can do to bless somebody.

Just me sitting,
  thinking about the golden opportunities that I've had
  and wondering what opportunity I can offer.

Just me sitting,
  thinking about Your glory,
  Your word and power
  and wondering who I can share this Good News with.

Just thinking about salvation
  and the life that You give
  and wondering who can I share it with.

Finally, brethren,
  whatsoever things are true,
  whatsoever things are honest,
  whatsoever things are just,
  whatsoever things are pure,
  whatsoever things are lovely,
  whatsoever things are of good report;
  if there be any virtue,
  and if there be any praise,
  think on these things
  and let them thrust you into action.

OH, SAY, CAN YOU SEE?

Can you see
The mounds of blessings
That are in front of you daily?

Can you feel the vibration
Of the voice of God
Saying you are my child,
You are special and amazing?

Can you hear
The triumph that's
Knocking at your door?

Can you taste
The success
That's waiting to be nibbled?

Can you smell
The greatness that's
On the inside of you?

Oh, can you see, feel, hear, taste, and smell
What your life can be?

Take in the blessings.
Feel the presence of God.
Hear the triumph.
Taste the success.
Smell your greatness,
Then live the phenomenal life
You were meant to live.
Oh, say, you must see!

God Can

YES, HE DID

He calmed the raging sea,
And He calmed me
When my emotions were raging.

He healed my sick body
When I couldn't imagine being well,
Or how that could happen.

He freed me from
The voices
That I heard in my head, daily
And gave me peace and silence.

He fed me
When I was hungry
And didn't have a dime.

He watched over me
When I was among enemies,
Without a friend.

He provided for me
When my utilities
Were about to be shut off.
He shut off the order
For the shut off.

He saved me
When I was a wretch undone.
He loved me
When I didn't love myself.

Yes, He did
Calm
Heal
Free
Feed
Watch over
Protect
Provide
Love and
Save me
And He can do the same for you.

Yes, He did!
Yes, He can.

HE NEVER

God ain't never rushed to do a thing.
I mean, never rushed to go anywhere,
Get things done, or make a decision.

God ain't never worried about anything.
He has a lot that He's responsible for—
The very hairs of your head are numbered.

God ain't never been concerned about haters.
He knows Who He is and He just do what He do.

God ain't never lied.
There's no need to.

He ain't never been late.
He's the master planner and scheduler.
If you consulted him,
He would be happy to give you some tips.
He knows the plans that he has for you.

He would be delighted to help you.
He got you.
He never, but He can.

Guidance

IT'S TIME

It's time for you to walk in the newness of life.
It's time for you to trust, believe and stop walking in fear.

Time to answer the call to your assignment,
Be quiet and still long enough to hear the call,
Get the assignment and the first instruction.

It's time to stop living in poverty and lack.
As a man thinketh in his heart, so is he.
The more you think about what you don't have, the more of
that you'll see.

It's time to stop talking about what you are going to do and do
it.
It's time to stop hiding your gifts and talents
And let the world see the beauty
And awesomeness of what you have to offer.

It's time to stop living in fear, poverty, lack; time to stop
talking and hiding.
But it's also time to walk, trust, be quiet, believe, listen,
And do what's deep in your heart to change your life
And the lives of others.

It's time to walk by faith
And not by sight.

LEAD ME LORD, LEAD ME

Lord, lead me to the path
Whereon I should walk.

Lead me to start walking
At the appropriate time
And nudge me
When it's time to stop.

Lord, when I stop,
Check on me
To see
If I'm in the right place.

When I arrive,
Direct me
To whom I should speak.
Give me the words,
The tone,
And the volume for delivery.

After speaking for the allotted time,
Give me the next instruction to follow.

Please walk with,
Guide, or carry me on this journey,
As you see and know what's up ahead.

When I arrive at the end of this journey,
For this appointed time,
Please give me
The wisdom, energy, strength, and everything

That I need for this phase in my life
To accomplish all that you have for me
In this time and space.

Thank you for your mercy and grace,
But please continue to lead me Lord,
Lead me.

MOMENT BY MOMENT

Lord, help me to trust in You
Moment by moment,
Hour by hour,
Day by day, all day, every day,
At all times, and in every circumstance.

Lord, moment by moment,
Hour by hour,
Day by day, all day, every day,
At all times, and in every circumstance,
Help me to treat everyone
With love and respect.

Lord, moment by moment,
Hour by hour,
Day by day, all day, every day,
At all times, and in every circumstance,
Help me to do what's right.

Lord, moment by moment,
Hour by hour,
Day by day, all day, every day,
At all times, and in every circumstance,
You are with me,
Guiding, leading, teaching, holding, upholding, protecting,
And taking care of me on every front.

So Lord, moment by moment,
Hour by hour,
Day by day, all day, every day,
At all times, and in every circumstance,

Help me to trust You,
Stay close to You,
Follow Your instructions,
Lean on You,
And believe that I can do all things,
As you give me strength,
Moment by moment.

LORD

Lord, use me to do your will,
To be your hands, eyes, and feet.

Lord, anoint me to speak only the words
That are fitting, profitable, and uplifting.

Give me the prayers to pray,
Privately when in an open forum
Or openly but privately for an individual.

Anoint my eyes to see
The beauty of the world,
Even when so many ugly things are happening,
And the beauty in someone's soul
When they don't know it's there.

Anoint my ears to hear the cries of those
Whose hearts are bleeding,
With no bandages available,
Nor a person to apply them.

Guide my steps to go to the places
Where You know my help,
Words, and assistance are needed.

Regulate my mind
To always put You first,
If I understand or not.

Let You be the first thought
and not the last resort.

Lord, I sacrifice my life for You,
so that I may live.

Lord, O Lord.

The Word of God

AMEN CHURCH

God is so good and His mercy endureth forever.
Amen church—Amen

The joy of the Lord is my strength.
Amen church—Amen

Praise God from Whom all blessings flow.
Amen church—Amen

Bless the Lord, O my soul, and all that is within me, bless His
holy name.
Bless the Lord, O my soul, and forget not all His benefits.
Let the church say amen—Amen

It is a good thing to give thanks unto the Lord and to sing
praises unto Thy name, O most high.
Amen church—Amen

Thou shall not commit adultery.
Amen church

Thou shall not kill.
Amen church

Thou shall not steal.
Amen church

Thou shall not covet (want what belongs to another) or lust.
Thou shall not lie and that includes the little white lies that
you tell.
Let the church say amen

Honor your father and mother.
Treat your parents with love and tenderness, and give them
respect.
Amen church

You are your brother's keeper.
You are to love your enemies.
You are to trust and obey.
Obedience is better than sacrifice.

Bring ye all the tithes into the storehouse.
Will a man rob God?
Give (even if it's a little) and it shall be given unto you,
Good measure, pressed down, shaken together,
And running over,
Shall men give into your bosom.
For with the same measure that ye mete withal,
It shall be measured to you again.

If you say amen or not.
If you believe it or not.
If you do it or not, the truth is the truth.

Let the church say amen.

HERE I AM GOD, IT'S ME AGAIN! - PART 1

Hi God, it's me, yeah, it's me again.
Didn't You say, "Come to me
All you who are weary and burdened,
And I will give you rest?"

Didn't You say, "Never will I leave you,
never will I forsake you?"

Didn't You say, not to be weary in doing good,
because at the proper time we will reap a harvest,
if we do not give up?

Doesn't the word say, You will be our glory?

Didn't David pray,
Lord, in You I have taken refuge;
Let me never be put to shame,
Deliver me in your righteousness.

Psalm 23 says, You can make us
Lie down in green pastures,
You lead us beside quiet waters.
Refresh our souls,
Guide us along the right paths.
Even when we walk through
The darkest valley we don't have to fear,
You comfort us.

You told Moses, "Now go,
I will help you speak and will teach you what to say."

Aren't you El, Eloah,
God Mighty, strong and prominent?
Aren't you Elohim, God, creator, mighty and strong?
Aren't you El Shaddai—God Almighty,
The ultimate power over all?
Aren't you Adonai—Lord?
Aren't you Yahweh/Jehovah?
The One who is present, accessible,
Near to those who call on You
For deliverance, forgiveness, and guidance?
Aren't you Jehovah Jireh,
The One who provides?
Aren't you Jehovah-Rapha,
The One who heals?
Aren't you Jehovah-Nissi,
The Lord our Banner who covers us?
Aren't you Jehovah-M'kaddesh,
The One who sanctifies and makes holy?
Aren't you Jehovah-Shalom,
The Lord our peace?

Jehovah-Elohim,
The Lord of Lords
Jehovah-Tsidkenu,
The Lord our righteousness
Jehovah Rohi,
The Lord our Shepherd
Jehovah Shammah,
The Lord who's there
Jehovah Sabaoth
The Lord of hosts,

The Host of both angels and of men.
The Host of heaven and the inhabitants of the earth.

Aren't You El Elyon,
The Most High?
El Roi,
The God that sees all
and see us in our distress?
El-Olam-the Everlasting God,
From everlasting to everlasting, you are God.
El-Gibhor—a mighty God,
A mighty warrior and champion.
You will destroy Your enemies
And rule with a rod of iron.
Nothing is too difficult for You.
You are authority over all,
You have great strength
And You always prevail.

HERE I AM GOD, IT'S ME AGAIN! - PART 2

You are my Rock, my Fortress, and Deliverer,
My shield, the Horn of my salvation,
My Stronghold in whom I can take refuge.

Didn't you say to Moses, "I Am That I Am?"
Which was a pledge and promise
That You would become whatever
They needed You to become.
And in this case, You became a Deliverer.

Well, God, tell me something.
If You are God, Lord, Jehovah Jireh, Rapha, Nissi,
El Shaddai, Jehovah Shammah, El Roi, Jehovah Shalom,
Rock, Fortress, Deliverer, and Shield,
Then nothing is too difficult for You.
You have great strength
And all authority is in Your hand.

So, why? Tell me why I feel so lost, sad, forgotten, beat down, useless, ashamed, weak, downtrodden, mad, angry, restless, unsure, unsafe, hungry, depressed, thirsty, poor, blind, empty, dumb, unhappy, alone, bound, so far away, bewildered, disgusted, afraid, confused, disappointed, frustrated, jealous, overwhelmed, stressed, troubled, worried, fearful, so full of shame, anxious, betrayed, distracted, disturbed, envious, guilty, and so resentful?
Tell me why, God?

You are all these things
And you are my Father.
Why am I in this position?
What can You say to me?
What can You do for me?

HERE I AM GOD, IT'S ME AGAIN! - PART 3

First of all, everything that you need
I have already provided.
But, do you believe that?
That's your first problem.
Not believing in Me enough
To know that I can be
And am everything that you need.

You don't believe that I created you,
A wonderful, beautiful, energetic, smart, strong, healthy,
vibrant, passionate, witty, brave, bright, charming, fabulous,
gentle, kind, pleasant, righteous, sincere, talented, vivacious,
thoughtful, capable, confident, efficient, wise, dashing and
dazzling, ambitious, honest, cheerful, helpful, credible and
incredible, debonair, courageous, cooperative, easy-to-entreat,
faithful, dynamic, patient, steadfast person,
Just to name a few of your qualities.

I created you and made you
In My image, reflecting My nature.
I gave you the responsibility
For the fish in the sea,
The birds in the air,
The cattle and every animal
That moves on the face of the earth
And yes, earth itself.
I told you to:
Prosper!

Reproduce!
Fill the earth!
Take charge!

So, if I did that and said that,
Don't you think I gave you
The intelligence, wisdom, courage,
Strength, bravery, ambition,
Health, patience, and energy
To get it done?

HERE I AM GOD, IT'S ME AGAIN! - PART 4

Well, you may say that was back in Bible times.
I say, I'm making people the same way
With blood, skin, cells, eyes, bones, and the senses.
So, what makes you anything less?

I've given you every sort of seed-bearing plant
and every kind of fruit bearing-tree for food,
Whatever grows out of the ground for food.
I'm still allowing things to grow.
You may not go outside and pick what you want,
But by faith I provide your food
And your finances for whatever you need.

You stopped believing in me
Because of a few minor afflictions,
A few problems and some setbacks.
I'm still the same today, yesterday, and forever.
"I Am That I Am."

Trust Me, believe in Me,
Have faith in Me and you'll see.
But when things come up, and they will,
Keep on believing and trusting
That I am your Jehovah Jireh.

As a man thinketh so is he.
Whatever you believe, that becomes your reality.
So, change your mind and change your life.

I am He who made heaven and earth.
I can do anything but fail.
You can do all things as I give you strength.

Here I am, God. Here You are.
Here we are together.

It's me again!
Saying thank you for teaching,
Loving, and being patient
As I live this wonderful and glorious life
That You gave me
In this amazing temple that You created.

THE WORD OF GOD

Stand up and praise the Lord your God,
    who is from everlasting to everlasting.

Blessed be Your glorious name,
    and may it be exalted above all blessing and praise.

You alone are the Lord.

You made the heavens,
    even the highest heavens
    and all their starry host,
    the earth and all that is on it,
    the seas and all that is in them.

You give life to everything
    and the multitudes of heaven worship You.

You are the Lord
    and You keep your promise,
    because You are righteous.

You made a name for Yourself,
    which remains to this day.

You divided the sea.

You led with a pillar of cloud
    and with a pillar of fire.

You spoke from
    and gave bread from heaven.

You brought forth water from a rock.

You said, Possess the land.

You are a forgiving God,
    gracious and compassionate,
    slow to anger,
    abounding in love,
    and in Your compassion,
    You deliver time after time.

You give your good spirit
    and instruction;
    You are patient and merciful.

You are God,
    great,
    mighty,
    good,
    awesome,
    and faithful,
    forever and ever.

Stand up and praise the Lord your God,
    who is from everlasting to everlasting.

Give Thanks

TAKE A MINUTE

Take a minute to
Thank God for waking you up today.

Take a minute to
Tell a friend or family member that you love them.

Take a minute to
Hold the door for someone coming in or going out.

Take a second to
Smile at someone as you walk pass them.

Take a minute to
Thank someone for giving you a helping hand,
Having your back, or
For moral support.

Take a minute to
Whisper a prayer.

Take a minute to
Breathe,
Laugh,
Stretch,
Eat,
Reflect,
Touch,
Feel,
Give,
Receive,
And to rest.

Take a few minutes to live and enjoy life.

Don't let everything pass you by,
Because you are so busy and forgetting to live.

Please take a minute!

AIN'T NO WAY

There ain't no way you can do what you do
    without some help and support:
    help from God,
    family, a friend, a co-worker, or a stranger.

There shouldn't be any way
    that you aren't saying thank you
    and thank you again.

When praises or thanks go up,
    you best believe
    that more blessings are coming down.

STOP!

Stop!
Just stop complaining
And start being thankful for what you have,
For being alive,
Even if you don't have everything you want.

Stop!
Just stop looking for fault and shortcomings in everybody
And be glad to have such precious souls in your midst.

Stop!
Just stop with your negative comments, commentary,
Self-righteous behavior,
Nobody can do it right but you,
Nobody can do it quite like you or as good as you.
Believe it or not,
Somebody's ideas and way of doing it are better than yours.

Stop!
Just stop talking about yourself,
Your accomplishments,
Your top position,
Your big-digits paycheck,
Your huge house,
Who you know,
Who you met,
Where you went,
Where you're going,
What you have,

And what you are going to get.
You didn't get there by yourself.

Stop!
Just stop talking about what you don't have,
How you never had a chance,
You never get a break,
You were overlooked,
You got messed around,
You got so close then the rug was snatched from under you.

Just stop!
It doesn't matter who, what, or when,
Because you can do anything you set your mind to do.
You can rise above your circumstances.

Stop!
Just stop, look around, and see the goodness,
The beauty, the blessings,
The people,
The opportunities,
The world,
Your family,
And your life.

Stop!
Just stop and say thank you.

Trust

THE TIME HAS COME

The time has come for me to move along.
To move to the next assignment,
Location,
Task,
Movement, or calling,
To the next group of people that I will influence,
Or who will influence, encourage, and support me.

I did my best, I've learned a lot.
I met some new people
And a new way to do some things.
I've laughed,
I've cried,
I've made mistakes and did some things well.
I tried to encourage,
Uplift, and support,
But if I fell short,
Please forgive me,
Because I really tried.

I'm not sure about what's coming next
Or who or when.
I just know that God has the perfect plan for me,
For my life, just for me.
Whatever it is, I'm sure it will be amazing,
Because God takes us from glory to glory.

I'm open to His leading and guiding,
He doesn't make mistakes and I trust Him.

I'm ready, God, do your thing.

DO YOU TRUST?
DO YOU OBEY?

Do you trust God?
Do you obey His Holy Word?
We say we trust God,
Then something unexpected happens
And we freak out.
It doesn't sound like a lot of trusting.

You call everybody—
Your neighbor, friend, your cousin and sister—
Everybody except God,
The one who can do something.

You finally remember God
After you've talked to many
And none could help.
You pray to God,
He drops in your heart and mind to do
One thing.
You've never done it before,
So you're skeptical and you don't do it.

Now you are confused,
Wondering what you should do.
You come to a conclusion
And make the decision to do that.

It works out okay,
But how marvelous it would have been
If you had trusted and obeyed God's way.

You would have pleased God
By trusting and obeying Him.

And when Daniel was lifted from the den no wound
was found on him,
Because he trusted in his God.

Eyes have not seen, nor ear heard,
Neither have entered into the heart of man,
The things which God hath prepared
For them that love Him (and trust Him).

Trust in the Lord with all your heart
And lean not on your own understanding;
In all your ways acknowledge Him,
And he will direct your paths.

Do you trust Him? Do you obey Him?

My Thoughts

JUST A MINUTE

Have you ever called someone in the next room?
And they said, just a minute.
Minutes pass,
Still the person doesn't come.

Has that happened with a phone call?
The person you're calling
Answers the phone.
Says I can't talk right now,
Can I call you back in a minute?
A minute, five minutes, an hour, a few hours,
A day, a few days go by
And you don't get a call back.

Wow!

What do you make of it?
They must be super busy,
They forgot,
Or something else came up.

Do you make promises that you don't keep?

Just a minute.
I'll call you tomorrow.
I'll get back to you in a few days.

People are busy these days.
You may be one of them.

So pay attention to your words,
Your promises
And your schedule,
Because you may be putting too much on it.

My mother told us,
Your word is your bond.

Let your word mean something,
So people will know
That they can trust in what you say
And depend on you.

You can be just a minute,
But if you need more,
Say so.

JUSTICE FOR ALL

Justice for all.
Really?
In what country, state, city, or school?
Justice for which race or culture?
Justice for what social class?
Justice for which gender?

Where is the justice
When you take a mother's child away
Because she is poor?

Where is the justice
When a man is locked up
because he is black?

Where is the justice
For the white man,
Who votes differently from you?

Do teens get proper justice?
Are Mexicans treated justly?
What about gays and lesbians?
Can the underdog find justice?
The person that society considers nobody,
Is there any justice for him?

Tell me who is treated fairly and justly?
Is it you or I?
Or only those in power, with money and influence?

I don't know.
If you know, tell me.
Does anyone know?
Or is that something that we need to talk about?

Justice for all.

WATCH OUT

Do you think Santa Claus is coming to town?

Someone may say,
"Watch out below!" when something is falling.

On a busy street one may yell,
"Watch out!" when a speeding vehicle is coming.

Do you hear "Watch out"
When your thinking is off?

Do you hear "Watch out"
When hanging out with people who don't dream or hope?

What about when
You stop believing in yourself
And you put more stock
Into what people are saying about you?

Do you hear "Watch out"
When you know you are going down the wrong path,
Wasting time, money, and energy?

What about lying,
Mistreating, and using people,
Or not being kind?

Watch out for the words coming from your lips
And the actions that you take.

So much to watch for, right?

Take off the blinders
And put your glasses on,
So you can see clearly
What to watch out for.

IF

If I could be anybody,
    who would I be?
    Would I be me
    or would I be you?

If I could say anything,
    would I speak my thoughts
    or would I say what I think you want me to say?

If I could sing any song,
    would I sing what's in my heart
    or would I sing the same old song?

If I could breathe,
    would I breathe
    or would I stop breathing,
    because you aren't breathing with me?

If I could go anywhere I wanted to go,
    would I go
    or would I stay home,
    because you weren't up for traveling?

If I could see and imagine anything,
    would I let my vision run wild
    or would I put on the blinders,
    because you think it is foolish
    and a waste of time to do that?

If I could help any person
    that I wanted to help,

would I help them
or would I let them suffer,
go without,
or fail
because you said, "What's the point?"

If I could live forever,
would I live or die
because you decided not to live?

Just saying. If.

WHAT DO YOU WANT? - NO. 1

What do you want out of life?
What do you expect?
Joy, happiness, contentment, love, peace, and respect

What are you giving?
Anger, criticism, judgment, condemnation, grief, complaints,
and disrespect

With whom are you sharing the above?
A spouse, child, neighbor, or friend

So let me make sure I have it right.
You want love, joy, happiness, peace, respect, and
contentment.

But you're giving
Criticism, judgement, grief, complaints, disrespect, anger, and
condemnation.

One plus one doesn't equal three.
What you are giving and what you are expecting will never add
up either.

If you want what you want, that's fine,
But your calculations need to change so they add up.
Change your ways so you can change your life.
Want what you want and get it.

What do you want?

WHATEVER, WHEREVER

Whatever you do, wherever you go, be present.
Be present so those around you will know
that they are important.
Give the situation and/or the person
your attention.

Turn off your cell phone,
Or at least put it on vibrate
And don't check it every other minute.
Focus on the subject at hand.

Give all and you will receive the same
Respect and courtesy in return.

Live with the attitude to respect all people
Regardless of race, finances, or background.

The people who are important to you,
Show them your love and let them love you.

Whatever, wherever.

IF WALLS COULD TALK

If walls could talk,
What would they say?
Would you listen?
Would you believe what you heard?
Would you talk,
Not knowing if what you said would be repeated?
Would you repeat what you heard?
Would you keep it to yourself?
We all know that walls can't talk,
But the people in those four walls can.
Watch what you say,
Don't believe everything that you hear,
And listen carefully.
Boy!
Man!
If walls could talk.

YOUR MIND, YOUR HEART

Do you listen to your mind
Or do you listen to your heart?
Your mind is telling you one thing
And your heart is telling you something else.
Which one sounds better?
Which one looks like the better outcome?
Which one makes more sense?
Which one is more secure?
Which do you believe will work?
Which one will your family, friend, or business partner go for?
Which feels better?
Which one can you see clearly in your mind's eye?
Do you wait for the mind and heart to agree with each other
Or do you just pick one?
There will be times when you can't figure it out.
But make sure you are using your mind
And your heart
And not the mind and heart
Of someone else.

ROSES AND OTHER THINGS

Roses are not only red.
Are violets blue?
Sugar comes in various colors and textures too.
Toilet tissue is not always soft.
Money isn't just green.
Salt isn't just for the table
Mats are not only for floors.
Gold is white, green, rose, strawberry, and blue—
Not only the golden shade that we are so familiar with.
Water is for drinking,
But there's a thousand other things to use it for.
You can sleep on a pillow, you can toss it,
You can use it to elevate
Or to alleviate pain.
All fire isn't destructive.

Are you rosy?
Are you blue?
Are you sweet?
Are you soft?
Are you green?
Are you salty?
Have you been floored?
Are you golden?
Are you thirsty?
Are you comfortable?
Are you on fire?
Or are you burning the candle at both ends?
You define your life,
Your goals, purpose, and mission:
Where you need to go,

What you need to do,
And who you want to be.
Let others define theirs,
Because your rose just may be red
And your violet may be blue.

HE SAID, SHE SAID—
WHAT DO YOU SAY?

He said, you are loud and out of control.
She said, I know that's right.

But I say, the Lord gave me this voice
And I am going to use it to testify of His goodness
And allow Him to control and use me,
And I say, thank you Lord.

She said, did you see that crazy outfit that she had on.
He said no, girl tell me about it.

I say, God made us all different.
He gave me the creativity that's in me.
I say, if God made us all different,
Why are we trying so hard to be like everybody else?

He said, she thinks that she can write and people will listen
to it.
She said, I know, I heard one of her pieces and I didn't get it.

I say, I can do all things through Christ who strengthens me.
If it's writing, sewing, baking, I can do it.
He or she that hath an ear to hear, let them hear.

She said, she can't carry a tune to save her life.
He said, I know, I heard her trying to sing in church last Sunday.

I say, make a joyful noise unto the Lord.
I say, God gave me a song that even the angels cannot sing.

He said, she said, but I say
I am the head and not the tail.
No weapon formed against me shall prosper.
I am a child of the most high God.
If God is for me, He is more than the world against me.

I am going to prosper and be in good health
Even as my soul prospers.
God is blessing me in all things, at all times.
God has plans to prosper me and to give me a hope and a
future.

He said, she said, but God said I am redeemed,
And I say, thank you God.

LITTLE BLACK GIRLS

Little black girls
Come in many shades:
Light, bright, caramel, chocolate, and dark chocolate.

Little black girls
Have various hair types:
Straight, wavy, curly, and kinky.

Little black girls
Have different parents,
Which gives each of them their own
Unique gifts, character, talents, personality, and values.

Little black girls
Like to play and have fun, learn, sing, act, dress up,
Go to the movies, to sleepovers, to hang out with friends,
Eat pizza and ice cream, play video games, talk on the phone,
Put on makeup, color, draw, have tea parties,
And so much more.

But be sure they all want and need
To be loved in the right way.

If you have a little black girl
Or if you know one, please
Love her,
Teach her to be polite, respectful, helpful, honest, kind,
Confident, and a go-getter.

Little black girls won't always be little.
One day they will be women
Who will influence other little black girls.

MUSIC

What's music to your ears?
You have a healthy baby boy or girl.
Your mom is going to be fine,
It was touch and go for a while,
But she is out of the woods and can go home.

Nothing is broken,
You are going to be sore for a few days,
But in a few weeks, you'll recover.

Mom I passed my exam this time,
But I studied for hours, thank you.

There has been some water damage,
But it's nothing that can't be repaired.

You're the best.
You have been chosen as employee of the year.

Some things are good to hear and some things not so much.

When we hear news that's not good,
We must find some music in our souls, hearts, and minds
To get us through the difficult times.

It may take a while, but the music will help light you up again
Whether it's within or without. Let it flow.
Don't feel like it's too soon if something on the inside is shining
out
Or if the music on the outside wants to shine in.

Listen to your music!

SO LONG, FAREWELL

Another year has come and gone and another one is here.

So long, farewell to all the time that I wasted,
The minutes, hours, days, weeks, and months.

So long, farewell to all the negative words that I spoke
And the blessings that I didn't count.

So long, farewell to my treatment of others
That wasn't positive or favorable.

So long, farewell to putting things off
And waiting for a better time.

So long, farewell to putting
Everyone's needs before my own.

So long, farewell to saying
I'm going to do better and use my time wisely.

I am going to speak
Whatsoever things are true, honest, just, pure, lovely and of
good report.

I am going to treat others the way I want to be treated;
With love, kindness, and respect
And count every single blessing regardless of its size.

I am going to jump on every opportunity
When prompted by the Holy Spirit!

I am going to help all whom I'm assigned to help,
But at the same time take care of myself.

I am going to do these things now
And do them every day
So at the end and close of this year
I won't have to have the same farewell speech.
It will be hello and thank you!

TIME

Time—we all have it.
Some a century, decades, years, months, weeks, days,
hours, minutes, seconds, milliseconds, microseconds,
nanoseconds, picoseconds or a jiffy.
How do you spend your time?
How will you spend your time?
How have you spent your time?
Your decade, year, month, week, day, and hour,
Your minute, second, millisecond, microsecond
Your nano- and picoseconds.
What about your jiffy?
We all spend time
Even if we don't plan to, intend to, or try to.
We spend time by default.
Whether you try or not, you are spending time
So why not make it count?
Make it count so when you are asked
Or when you think about it you will
Know that you spent your time wisely:
Praying
Helping others
Following and achieving your dream
Working on yourself and making improvements
Traveling and enjoying life, spreading love, sharing your riches
Encouraging those in your path, being the best you
Learning, getting good, getting better, and being the best
Letting go of your hurts, prejudice, condemnation, criticism,
judgment, unforgiveness,
And the list could go on.
Make this jiffy, picosecond, hour, day, week, year, decade
count.

Make it your best time.
Let time work for you,
Because if you spend it or not,
You are still spending it.
This is your time!
Now!

TWENTY-FIVE CENTS

Twenty-five cents is one quarter
Twenty-five cents is also two dimes and a nickel
Twenty-five cents can be five nickels
Twenty-five cents is one dime and three nickels
Twenty-five cents is twenty-five pennies
Twenty-five cents is two dimes and five pennies
Twenty-five cents is one dime and fifteen pennies
Twenty-five cents is one dime, ten pennies, and one nickel
Twenty-five cents is fifteen pennies and two nickels
Twenty-five cents is ten pennies and three nickels
Twenty-five cents is five pennies, one dime, and two nickels
Twenty-five cents is fifteen pennies and one dime
You may figure out more, but that's as far as I'm going with it.
When Freddy (my son) was a small boy,
He thought the more coins that you had, the more money you had.
If you gave him a case quarter
He would get upset and want the twenty-five pennies.
You could also give him ten pennies instead of a quarter
Because he thought the ten pennies was more.
What are you accepting because it looks like more?
Someone handsome or beautiful on the outside
Who doesn't have a single bit of integrity;
Someone smart, brilliant, funny, or fun
Who is wrapped up in what they think is important;
Someone loaded who couldn't care less
If you have bread or milk;
Someone who can sing like a songbird
But never bother to listen to your words or song;
Someone who lights up the room when he walks in
But always seems to snuff your light out;

144

Someone who can cook her butt off but never offer you a meal;
Someone who has the finest car that money can buy
But to this day hasn't let you put your behind on the seat;
Someone who has a home that is out of sight
But never invited you in out of the cold, sun, or rain;
Someone who is a magnet for success
But never dropped a nugget of wisdom on you.
Don't be fooled by what looks like more,
Because it may be the same or less—
Twenty-five cents is just twenty-five cents.

WHAT DO I CHOOSE?
YOU DECIDE

What do I choose?
Do I choose day or night?
Do I choose dark over light?
Do I choose black or white?
Do I choose right over wrong?
Do I stay silent or do I sing my song?
Do I choose the sun over the moon?
Do I choose the stars over the seas?
Do I choose the mountain over the valley?
Do I choose to walk or run?
Do I choose yes or no?
Do I choose to sit or stand?
Do I sleep or watch TV?
Every single day I have to decide.
Every day you have to decide.
What do I consider when making my choices?
Do I flip a coin?
Do I draw a straw?
Do I pick something, just to get it over with?
Do I consult with someone?
Do I pray about it?
Do I ponder and try to make the best possible decision based
on my needs?
Do I factor in the needs of others before I choose?
Do I throw up my hands and say what difference does it make?
Do I think it doesn't matter, who cares, or who gives a flying
fart?
Whatever you choose, whenever you choose,

You will be affected and those close to you will be impacted.
People you don't even know may be affected by your decision.

Sometimes it is all about you, what you need, want, and desire.
Sometimes it's not about you at all, but other people.
What do I choose?
How do I choose?
When do I choose?
Where do I choose?
It may not be simple or easy.
Yet, you choose, you decide, and I'll choose, I'll decide,
Or do I choose, but you really decide?

WHAT DO YOU WANT? - NO. 2

What do you want from me, yourself,
And the world?

What do you want from your spouse or children:
Love and respect?
Well, it's not fair
When you never have anything good
Or encouraging to say to them.

What do you want and expect from your employer:
A raise or a promotion?
How is that, when you're not a very good employee?

What do you want and expect from your friends:
Support, love, a listening ear, encouragement, sharing a meal
from time to time?
It's not fair when you don't give support or love,
You never have time to share a meal,
You are so focused on your hurts and woes
That you can't hear or don't want to hear what's going on in
their lives.
You never say anything good.

What do you need and expect from the world:
Good health, prosperity, peace, happiness, joy, love, and
understanding?

Dear lady and kind sir,
If you want gifts from the world,
You have to take part.

You have to do what makes a healthy body.
For prosperity you have to give something.
Give without looking for a return.
Give, even if it's a little.
Give, and it will be given unto you.

You will receive peace, happiness, joy,
Love, understanding, and financial blessings.

So, tell me, what do you really want?

LESSONS LEARNED

Have you ever responded to someone's question
With the wrong answer?
And they burst into laughter,
Right in your face.
It's a lesson learned.

Have you been called on in class,
Even when you didn't raise your hand?
You weren't sure about the answer,
But the answer that you gave was correct.
It's a lesson learned.

Have you ever taken a test
That you studied hard and long for?
You weren't sure how much of the information you retained.
You took the test and passed it with flying colors.
It's a lesson learned.

You had a test coming up,
But you didn't study.
You told yourself,
I know that stuff.
You took the test
And you failed.
Guess what,
It's a lesson learned.

Have you ever worked on a project
But were too stubborn or too full of pride to ask
Someone for help?
You thought they wouldn't be willing to advise you.

You later realized that they had information ready for you.
You never asked, so, they didn't interfere.
It's a lesson learned.

You have information at your fingertips
That you could share with someone,
Which would have been helpful to them.
You didn't and the project blew up in their face.
It's a lesson learned.

Did you ever doubt yourself and were afraid to try?
You launched out into the deep
And to your surprise, you were successful.
It's a lesson learned.

Have you had someone stare at you?
Which made you wonder, what is their problem?
You understand later.
They were admiring how beautiful and together you are.
Another lesson learned.

Every day we learn lessons.
At least, every day we should be learning lessons.
Pay attention.
Lighten up.
Get over the hurt, shock, or surprise.
Forgive the person, even though they didn't ask you to.
If necessary, talk to the person.

Continue to love and see what lessons you need to learn.

WHY DO I?

Why do I laugh
When there isn't a single thing funny?
Why do I cry
When someone says or does something to hurt my feelings?
Why do I lie
When there is no reason to?
Why do I tell the truth
When it will get me in a world of trouble?
Why do I frown
When I see someone of a different culture or race?
Why do I smile
When I see a complete stranger?
Why do I withhold love and compassion
From family, friends, or neighbors?
Why do I give time, money, and energy
To people on the other side of the world?
Why do I put on a happy face
When you've hurt me to my core?
Why do I act so unhappy
When you are giving me everything that you've got?
Why do I sit
When the music is playing?
Why do I dance
When there isn't any music playing at all?
Why do I complain
When I have everything that I want?
Why do I sing
When tragedy is all around me and there's nothing to sing about?
Why do I overeat?
Why do I say I'll go to the gym tomorrow?

Why do I sit and watch TV for hours?
Why do I not get my work done,
Then rush around at the last minute?

Why do I?
Why do you?
Why do we?

We all have our why do I statements.

We all have our work to do and improvements to make.

When will you, I, we start doing the work to make our lives,
The lives of others, and this world a better place?

Why?

When?

Holidays

HAPPY MOTHER'S DAY

Happy Mother's Day to all of the moms, grandmas, great-grandmas, great-great-grandmas, stepmothers, mothers-in-law, foster moms, mothers in the faith, and all others.

Today is the day that we celebrate women of different races, classes, ages, and cultures.
Today is the day that is set aside to say thank you.
Thank you for loving, caring for, teaching, guiding, feeding, and protecting me.

Today is the day that we show gratitude, buy gifts, send flowers and cards, go out to eat, talk, and spend time together.

Cherish your time together, but not just on Mother's Day.
Make the time that you spend together count and the gifts you give meaningful.
Be present and helpful when necessary and/or possible.

God gave us mothers and wants us to honor them.
Your mother may not be here today, but honor the memory that you have, even if it's only the day that she gave you life.

God is pleased when we love our neighbor, but I think he is especially happy and proud when we love, honor, and respect our mothers.

So Happy Mother's Day to all the moms, grandmothers, sisters, aunts, nieces, cousins, in-laws, wives, daughters, friends, and neighbors.
May God bless you all.

HAPPY BIRTHDAY, JESUS

Do you know anyone who had a birthday party and everybody got gifts except the person whose birthday was being celebrated?

That's what we do, every year, to Jesus. We buy gifts for family, friends, co-workers, bosses, people we like, and people we don't like.

Who does that? Most of us. We run around frantically. Some walk calmly. We max out our credit cards. We try to remember everyone on the list, then we remember people we forgot to put on the list. We bake, we decorate, we have or attend parties. We overeat, we drink too much, we travel, we send cards, and we give all kinds of gifts, usually expecting one in return.

Whew! We don't have to do it—at least, we don't have to do it all. It's not their birthday and it's not yours. We make ourselves sick, broke, and weary when we don't need to. Plus, you still didn't get a gift for the one whose birthday we're celebrating.

If you got Him a gift, you could save yourself a lot of time, money, and energy. The gift that He wants is love. Love Him, love your neighbor and yourself. Price tag free! Free for all. Free to give and free to receive.

It's Christmas and your traditions don't have to change, unless you want them to. But please remember to give a gift to the One whom we are supposed to be celebrating. That gift is love—love to all, every day, and not just on Christmas.

Happy Birthday, Jesus.

ABOUT THE AUTHOR

Darlene Davis is a poet, a lover of people, and a wife to Fred. She has a special place in her heart for children, youth, and the young at heart. She writes with inspiration from God to motivate, uplift, encourage, and to cheer on the reader.

Darlene was raised in a Christian home with a large family. She is a wife of 43 years, a mother, grandmother, and a great-grandmother. She has always been someone whom family members turn to for a word of encouragement or a listening ear.

She has a blog with a new message every Sunday for her readers. You can find it at www.myinspirationforyou.com. You can email her at doubledhisheart@gmail.com. She would love to hear from you.

Made in the USA
Columbia, SC
26 December 2019